PIANO

Adventures® *by Nancy and Randall Faber*

A BASIC PIANO METHOD

An alphabetical listing of pieces is on the inside back cover.

Production: Frank and Gail Hackinson

Production Coordinator: Marilyn Cole

Editors: Victoria McArthur and Edwin McLean

Cover and Illustrations: Terpstra Design, San Francisco

Engraving: Fallström Ltd., Hollywood, Florida

Printer: Tempo Music Press, Inc.

THE
F·J·H
MUSIC
COMPANY
INC.

Frank J. Hackinson

CONTENTS

Sitting at the Piano

1. Are you seated the correct **DISTANCE** from the keyboard?

2. Are you seated the correct **HEIGHT** at the piano?

3. Are you **SITTING TALL** yet relaxed?

Check yourself:

Sit straight and tall on the
front part of the bench.
With arms straight, your knuckles should
reach the fallboard. If you have to lean,
move the bench forward or backward.

Check yourself:

With your hands on the keys, your arms
should be level with the keyboard. If
not, you may need to sit on a cushion
or book.

Check yourself:

Is your back straight?
Shoulders relaxed?
Can you easily take a deep breath?

This is your position for playing the piano.

Hand Position

Keeping your fingers straight, hold your hands out in front of you.
Notice the fingers are all different lengths.

straight

Now relax and **round the hand.**

Magic! Now your fingers are all
the same length.

curved

Notice how your hand
makes the letter "C".

**It is important to keep a relaxed, curved hand position
as you play the piano.**

Finger Numbers

Each finger has a number!

L.H.
stands for
Left Hand.

R.H.
stands for
Right Hand.

Finger Drill:

On the closed keyboard and with a rounded hand position -

1. Tap both finger **1's.**
2. Tap both finger **2's.**
3. Tap both finger **3's.**
4. Tap both finger **4's.**
5. Tap both finger **5's.**
6. Tap R.H. finger **1.**
7. Tap L.H. finger **5.**
8. Tap L.H. finger **2.**
9. Tap R.H. finger **4.**
10. Tap R.H. finger **2.**

Playing on the White Keys

The keys on the piano are black and white.
We call all of the keys on the piano the **KEYBOARD**.

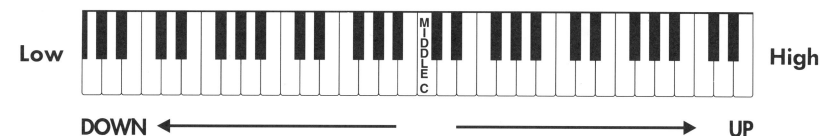

Low

MIDDLE C

High

DOWN ⟵   ⟶ UP

The Pecking Hen

FOR RIGHT HAND ON WHITE KEYS

Put your thumb behind your 3rd finger to help give you a good hand position.

Start in the **middle** of the piano. Using your 3rd finger (braced with the thumb) play all the white keys going HIGHER – to the right.
This is going **UP the keyboard**.

Listen to how the keys sound! When the keys are higher, the sound is higher.

The Pecking Rooster

FOR LEFT HAND ON WHITE KEYS

Put your thumb behind your 3rd finger to help give you a good hand position.

Start in the **middle** of the piano. Using your 3rd finger (braced with the thumb) play all the white keys going LOWER – to the left.
This is going **DOWN the keyboard**.

Listen to how the keys sound! When the keys are lower, the sound is lower.

Theory p. 3   Technique p. 5

Teacher Note: For good technique, encourage the student to *drop* into the 2-black-keys as fingers 2 and 3 play together.

Two Black Ants

Black keys are in groups of

2's and 3's.

Can you find these on the piano?

Use **Left Hand fingers 2 and 3.**
Play on the 2-black-key groups.

(Your teacher will demonstrate.)

L.H.

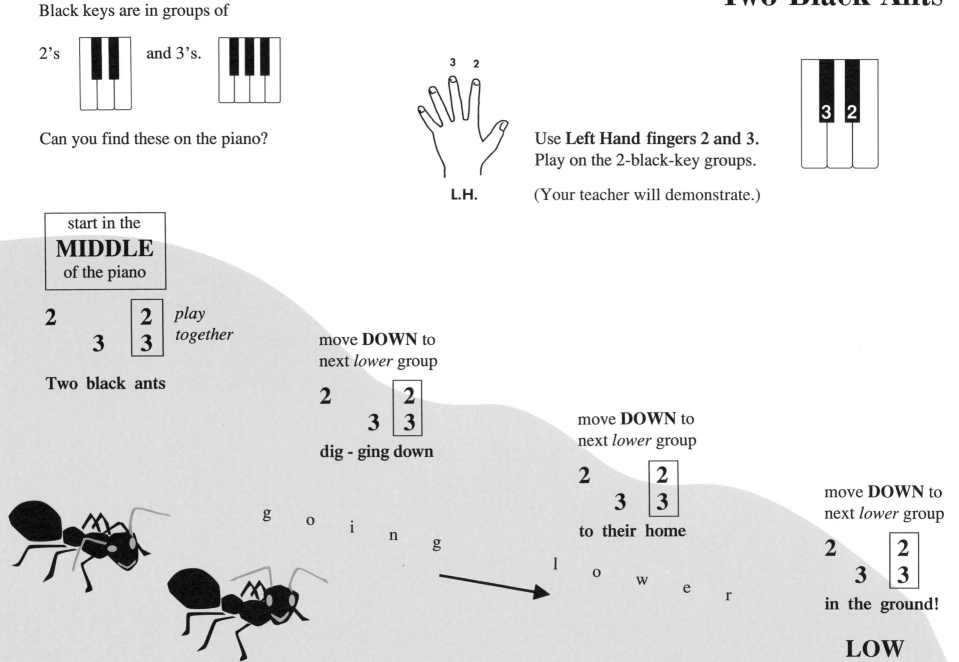

start in the
MIDDLE
of the piano

2
  3

| 2 |
| 3 |

play together

Two black ants

move **DOWN** to
next *lower* group

2
  3

| 2 |
| 3 |

dig - ging down

g o i n g

move **DOWN** to
next *lower* group

2
  3

| 2 |
| 3 |

to their home

l o w e r

move **DOWN** to
next *lower* group

2
  3

| 2 |
| 3 |

in the ground!

LOW

Two Blackbirds

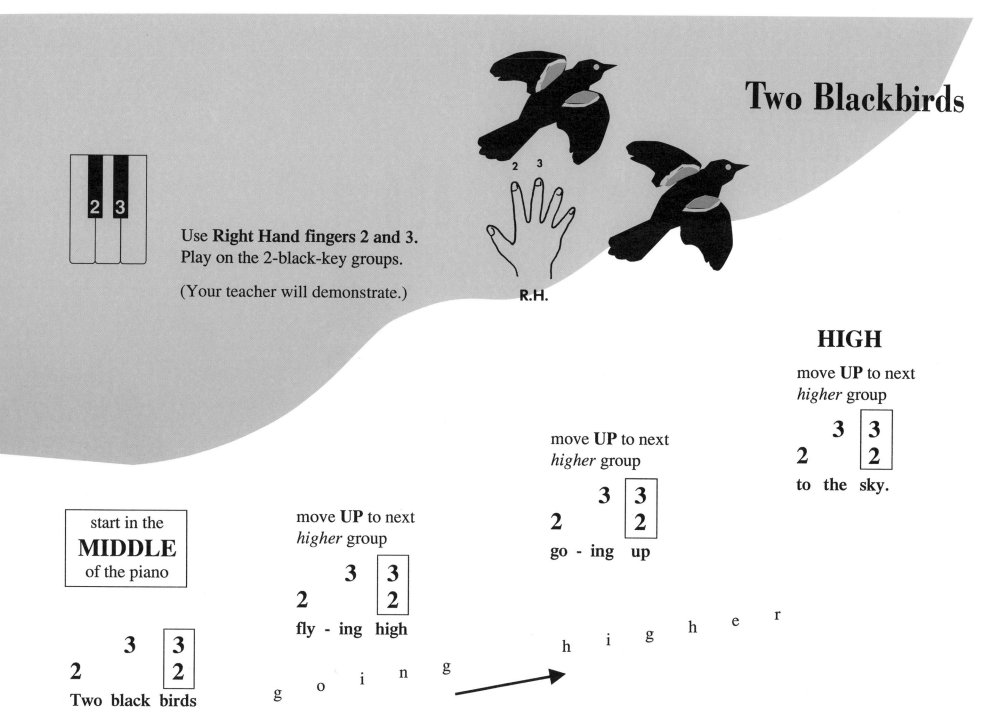

Use **Right Hand fingers 2 and 3.**
Play on the 2-black-key groups.

(Your teacher will demonstrate.)

R.H.

HIGH

move **UP** to next
higher group

	3	**3**
2		**2**

to the sky.

move **UP** to next
higher group

	3	**3**
2		**2**

go - ing   up

move **UP** to next
higher group

	3	**3**
2		**2**

fly - ing   high

start in the
MIDDLE
of the piano

	3	**3**
2		**2**

Two   black   birds

g   o   i   n   g   h   i   g   h   e   r

Technique p. 4, 5

Into the Cave

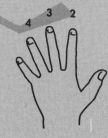

4 3 2

L.H.

Use **Left Hand Fingers 2, 3 and 4.**.
Play on the 3-black-key groups.

(Your teacher will demonstrate.)

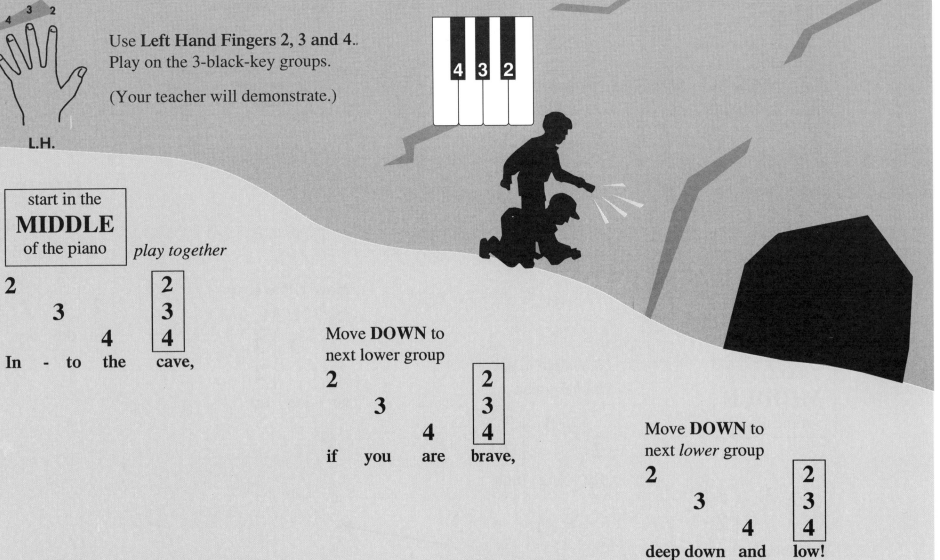

4 3 2

start in the
MIDDLE
of the piano   *play together*

2
   3
      4   2 3 4

In - to the cave,

Move **DOWN** to
next lower group

2
   3
      4   2 3 4

if you are brave,

Move **DOWN** to
next *lower* group

2
   3
      4   2 3 4

deep down and low!

LOW

Teacher Reminder: Encourage the student to *drop* into the 3-black-keys as fingers 2-3-4 play together.
When demonstrating, the teacher might say, "2-3-4 drop and lift.".

Three Little Kittens

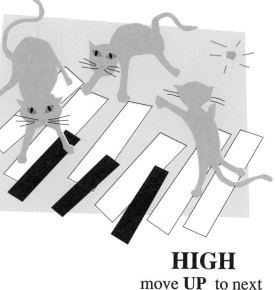

 Use **Right Hand Fingers 2, 3 and 4**.
Play on the 3-black-key groups.

(Your teacher will demonstrate.)

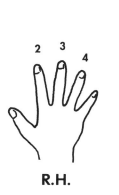

R.H.

HIGH
move **UP** to next
higher group

4
3
2

MEOW!

move **UP** to next
higher group

4 | 4 |
  3 | 3 |
2 | 2 |

play - ing   the   keys,

move **UP** to next
higher group

4 | 4 |
  3 | 3 |
2 | 2 |

cute   as   can   be,

start in the
MIDDLE
of the piano

4 | 4 |
  3 | 3 |
2 | 2 |

Kit - tens   are   we,

 CREATIVE

Compose (make up) a short piece of your own using the 3-black-keys.
Call it "The Roller Coaster." Start *low* and make the roller coaster
climb *high,* then come back down again. Give your fingers a fun ride!

Performance p. 2   Theory p. 4   Technique p. 4, 5

The Quarter Note

Music, like your body, has a steady "heartbeat".
The **beat** can be slow, medium, or fast, but must always be **steady**.

The Quarter Note

= 1 count
(or beat)

Tap on your lap
and count aloud:

1	1	1	1
or Ta	Ta	Ta	Ta

Choose any key on the piano and play the quarter notes. Count aloud.
Keep the beat steady - like a clock ticking in perfect time!

Counting correctly and keeping a steady beat gives us RHYTHM.

If your teacher has a metronome, ask if you may tap your ♩'s to the steady
tick of the metronome.

Draw 3 quarter notes for the right hand.
Notice the stem goes up on the right side.
Write **"1"** below each note.

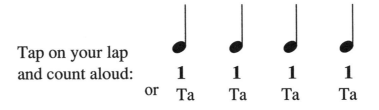

Ex. ___1___ count   _____ count   _____ count   _____ count

Draw 3 quarter notes for the left hand.
Notice the stem goes down on the left side.
Write **"1"** below each note.

Ex. ___1___ count   _____ count   _____ count   _____ count

Practice Suggestions

1. Before playing, tap the rhythm on your lap using a rounded hand position.
   Use the correct hand to tap each line.
2. Play and count "one, one", or "ta, ta", etc.
3. Play and chant the words.
4. Play in different places on the piano.
   Tell your teacher if you are playing *high*, *low* or *in the middle* of the piano.

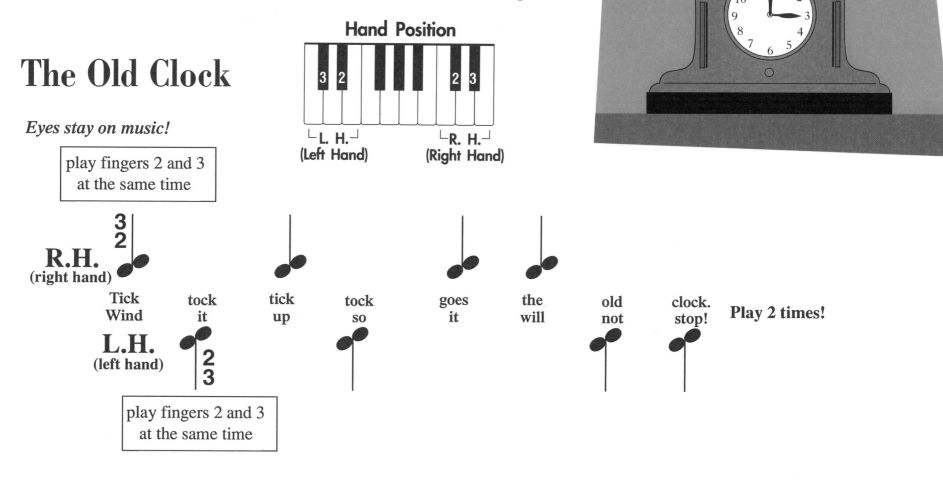

The Old Clock

Eyes stay on music!

Hand Position

play fingers 2 and 3 at the same time

R.H. (right hand)

Tick — tock — tick — tock — goes — the — old — clock. **Play 2 times!**
Wind — it — up — so — it — will — not — stop!

L.H. (left hand)

play fingers 2 and 3 at the same time

Teacher Duet: (student plays *in the middle* of the keyboard)

Practice Suggestions

1. On the closed piano lid, play and say the finger numbers aloud.
2. On the piano, play and count "one, one" or "ta, ta", etc.
3. Play and sing the words.
4. Play in different places on the piano.

Hand Position

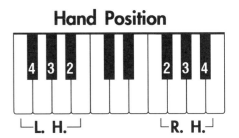

└ L. H. ┘   └ R. H. ┘

The Walking Song

Finger Check: *Do you have a rounded hand position?*

repeated note

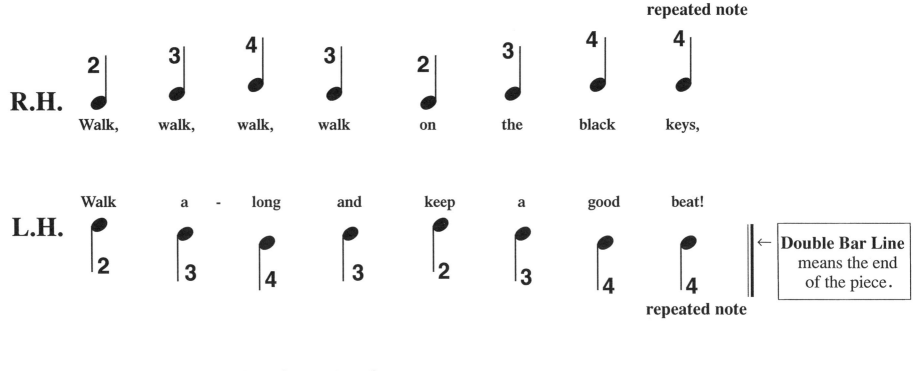

R.H.

| 2 | 3 | 4 | 3 | 2 | 3 | 4 | 4 |

Walk, walk, walk, walk on the black keys,

Walk a - long and keep a good beat!

L.H.

| 2 | 3 | 4 | 3 | 2 | 3 | 4 | 4 |

repeated note

← **Double Bar Line** means the end of the piece.

Teacher Duet: (Student plays *in the middle* of the keyboard)

Practice Suggestions

1. Play and say finger numbers.
2. Play and count "one, one", or "ta, ta", etc.
3. Play and sing the words.
4. Play in different places on the piano.

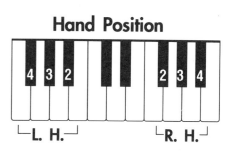

Hand Position

L. H.   R. H.

Eye Check: *Are your eyes on the music and not on your hands?*

Two Questions

repeated note
(same finger)

R.H.

2		3		4		3	
Is	your	hand	po	- si -	tion	read	- y?

L.H.

Are	your	quar	- ters	al	- ways	stead	- y?
2	*(same finger)*	3		4			

DISCOVERY Circle each repeated note.

Teacher Duet: (Student plays *in the middle* of the keyboard)

mp

Theory p. 6

The Half Note

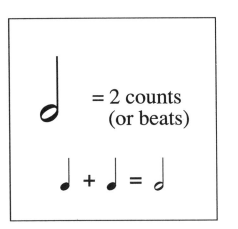

♩ = 2 counts
(or beats)

♩ + ♩ = 𝅗𝅥

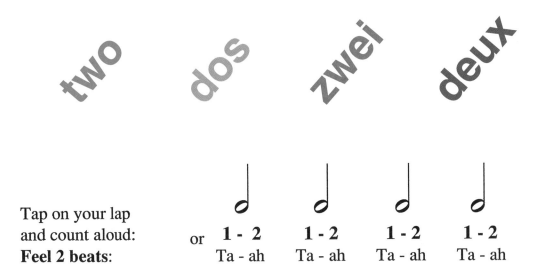

Tap on your lap
and count aloud:
Feel 2 beats:

or   **1 - 2**   **1 - 2**   **1 - 2**   **1 - 2**
     Ta - ah   Ta - ah   Ta - ah   Ta - ah

Choose any key on the piano and play the half notes. Count aloud.
Keep a steady beat!

Your teacher may let you tap your 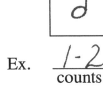's to the steady tick of the metronome.

Draw 3 half notes for the right hand.
Remember, the stem goes up on the right side.
Write **"1-2"** below each note.

Ex.   <u>1-2</u>   <u>1-2</u>   <u>1-2</u>   <u>1-2</u>
      counts   counts   counts   counts

Draw 3 half notes for the left hand.
Remember, the stem goes down on the left side.
Write **"1-2"** below each note.

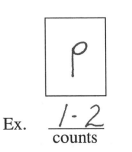 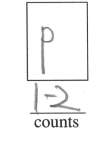 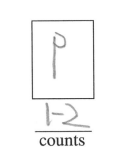 

Ex.   <u>1-2</u>   <u>1-2</u>   <u>1-2</u>   <u>1-2</u>
      counts   counts   counts   counts

Practice Suggestions

1. Tap the rhythm on your lap using a rounded hand position.
   Use the correct hand to tap each line.
2. Play and say finger numbers.
3. Play and count.
4. Play and sing the words.

Continue to use these practice suggestions for the pieces that follow in this book.

The I Like Song

Hand Position

Performance p. 3   Technique p. 6, 7

Music is made more interesting with loud and soft sounds.

Forte (f) means loud.   **Piano** (p) means soft.

Circle the f and p signs in the music!

Hand Position

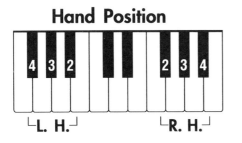

I Hear the Echo

Finger Check: *Ask your teacher to check your hand position.*

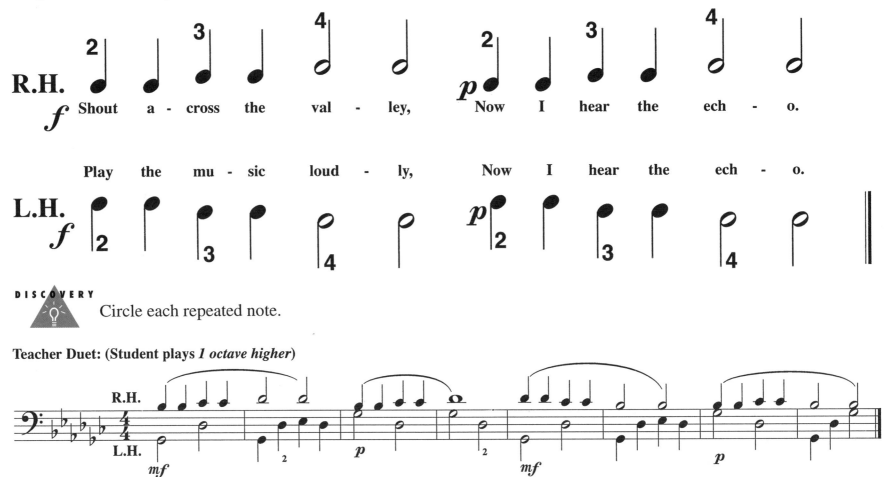

R.H.

f Shout a - cross the val - ley, p Now I hear the ech - o.

Play the mu - sic loud - ly,   Now I hear the ech - o.

L.H.

DISCOVERY Circle each repeated note.

Teacher Duet: (Student plays *1 octave higher*)

FF1   FF1

The Whole Note

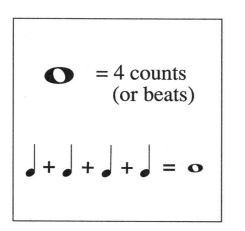

o = 4 counts
(or beats)

♩ + ♩ + ♩ + ♩ = o

Tap on your lap
and count aloud:
Feel 4 beats:

or

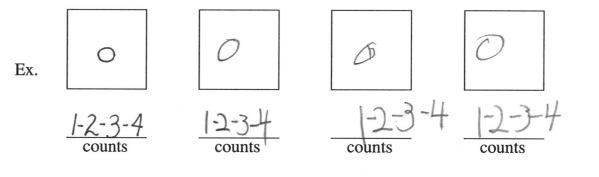

o   **o**
1 - 2 - 3 - 4   **1 - 2 - 3 - 4**
Ta - ah - ah - ah   Ta - ah - ah - ah

Choose any key on the piano and play the whole notes. Count aloud.
KEEP THE BEAT STEADY!

Draw 3 whole notes.
Notice there is no stem.
Write **"1-2-3-4"** below each note.

Ex.

1-2-3-4	12-3-4	1-2-3-4	12-3-4
counts	counts	counts	counts

Rhythm Drill

Choose any key on the piano and play the rhythm below. Notice the *f* and *p* signs. Play it with the R.H., then the L.H.
(Perhaps your teacher will let you use the metronome.)

o   o   ♩ ♩ ♩ ♩ ♩   ♩
f   *p*   *f*   *p*

Theory p. 9

Practice Suggestions

1. Tap the rhythm on your lap with a rounded hand position. Use the correct hand to tap each line.
2. Play and say finger numbers.
3. Play and count.
4. Play and sing the words.
5. Play *Old MacDonald* in different places on the keyboard.

Hand Position

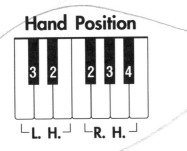

└ L. H. ┘ └ R. H. ┘

Old MacDonald Had a Song

Eye Check: *Ask your teacher to watch your eyes as you play. Did you have to look down?*

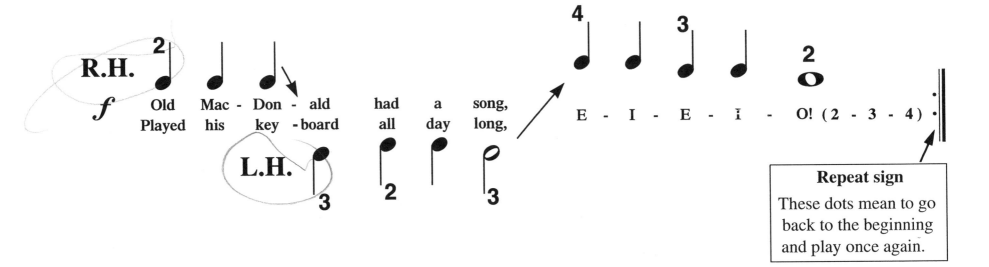

R.H.

2

f

Old   Mac - Don - ald   had   a   song,
Played   his   key - board   all   day   long,

L.H.   3   2   3

4   3   2

E - I - E - ĭ - O! (2 - 3 - 4)

Repeat sign
These dots mean to go back to the beginning and play once again.

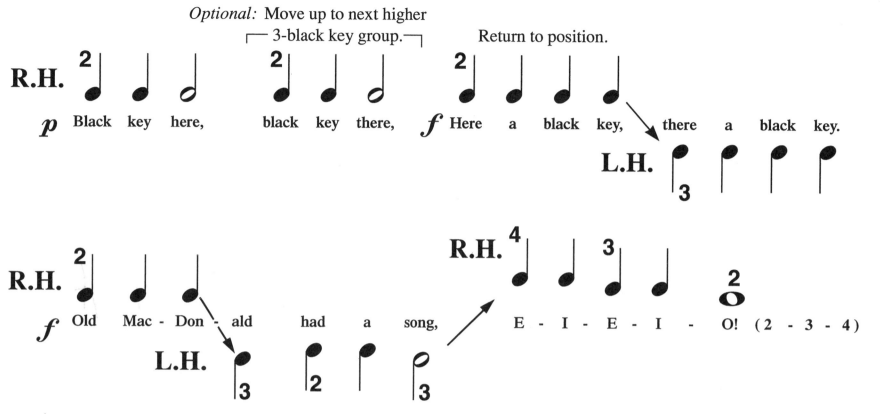

Optional: Move up to next higher
⌐—3-black key group.—⌐ Return to position.

R.H. *p* Black key here, black key there, *f* Here a black key, there a black key.

L.H.

R.H. *f* Old Mac-Don-ald had a song, E - I - E - I - O! (2 - 3 - 4)

L.H.

R.H.

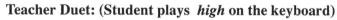

CREATIVE Compose a short piece that uses only *whole notes*. Call it "Two Slow-Walking Turtles." Use only the L.H. and play *low* on the keyboard.

Teacher Duet: (Student plays *high* on the keyboard)

R.H.

L.H. *mf* *p*

cresc. *mf*

Technique p. 8, 9

The Music Alphabet

Each white key has a name that comes from the music alphabet.

The music alphabet has 7 letters: **A B C D E F G**

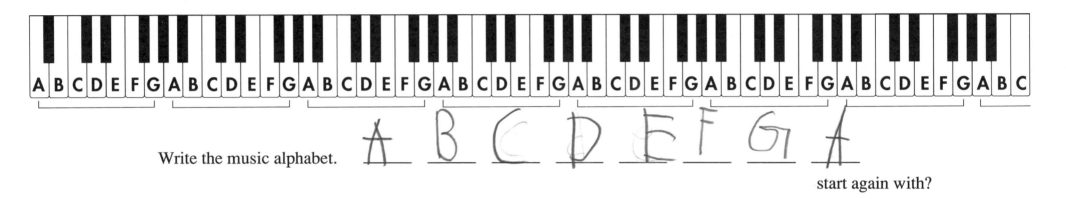

Write the music alphabet.   A   B   C   D   E   F   G   A

start again with?

    Use the third finger supported by the thumb.
(L.H. plays the lower notes, R.H. plays the higher notes.)

Alphabet Drill

1. **Play** and **say** the white keys starting with the lowest key, **A**, and ending with the highest key, **C**.

2. Practice finding **G's**.
   (Find a group of 3 black keys. G is the white key between the first and second black keys.)

3. Beginning on any **G**, **play** and **say** the music alphabet *going down*.   **A B C D E F G**
   Play 3 times: *high*, in the *middle*, and *low* on the piano.   ⟵

Learning C-D-E

(the 3 white keys surrounding
the 2 black-key-group)

C D E

Circle all the groups of 2-black-keys on the keyboard below.
Then print **C-D-E** on the surrounding 3 white keys.

Ex.

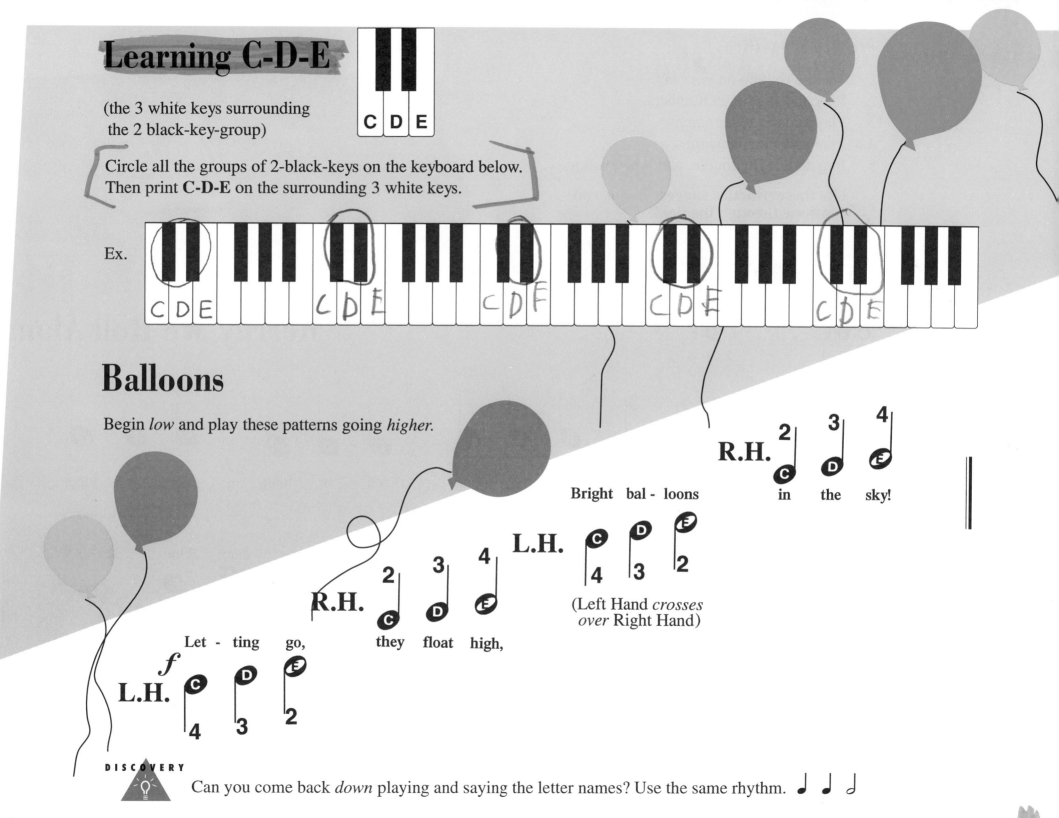

Balloons

Begin *low* and play these patterns going *higher.*

R.H. C D E
in the sky!

Bright bal - loons

L.H. C D E
(Left Hand *crosses
over* Right Hand)

R.H. C D E
they float high,

L.H. *f* C D E
Let - ting go,

DISCOVERY

Can you come back *down* playing and saying the letter names? Use the same rhythm.

Practice Suggestions

1. Tap the rhythm on your lap.
2. Play and say finger numbers.
3. Play and say letter names.
4. Play and sing the words.
5. Play in a high, middle, and low position.

Use these practice suggestions as you continue through the book.

Merrily We Roll Along

Mer - ri - ly we roll a - long, roll a - long, roll a - long.

Mer - ri - ly we roll a - long, o'er the deep blue sea!

DISCOVERY Look at the music with your teacher. Where do the notes **move down**, **move up**, **repeat**?

Teacher Duet: (Student plays *high* on the keyboard)

Learning F-G-A-B

(the 4 white keys surrounding the 3-black-key group)

F G A B

Circle all the groups of 3-black-keys on the keyboard below.
Then print **F-G-A-B** on the surrounding 4 white keys.

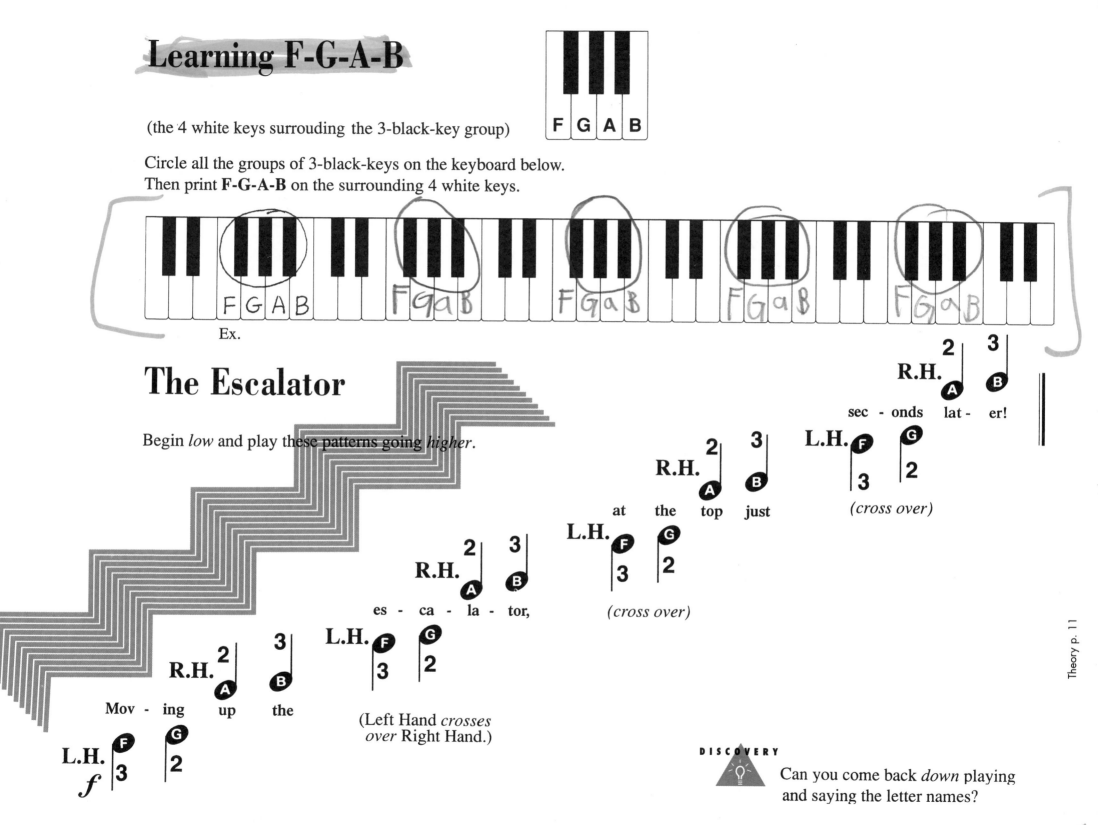

The Escalator

Begin *low* and play these patterns going *higher*.

L.H. F G
f 3 2

R.H. A B
2 3

Mov - ing up the

L.H. F G
3 2

(Left Hand *crosses*
over Right Hand.)

R.H. A B
2 3

es - ca - la - tor,

L.H. F G
3 2

(cross over)

R.H. A B
2 3

at the top just

L.H. F G
3 2

(cross over)

R.H. A B
2 3

sec - onds lat - er!

DISCOVERY

Can you come back *down* playing
and saying the letter names?

Theory p. 11

About Steps

A **STEP** moves to the **next key** 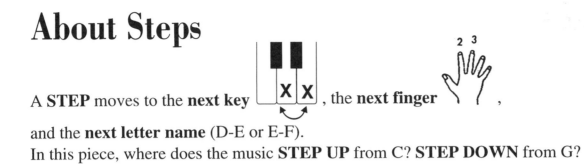 , the **next finger** ,

and the **next letter name** (D-E or E-F).
In this piece, where does the music **STEP UP** from C? **STEP DOWN** from G?

C-D-E-F-G March

C Position

L.H.   R.H.

C D E F G   C D E F G
5 4 3 2 1   1 2 3 4 5

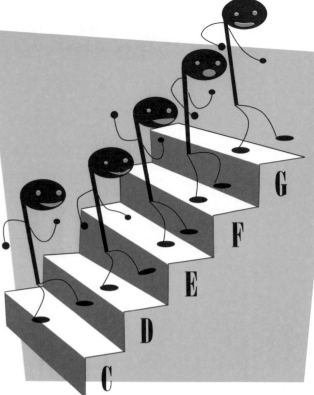

Which hand begins this piece? ___

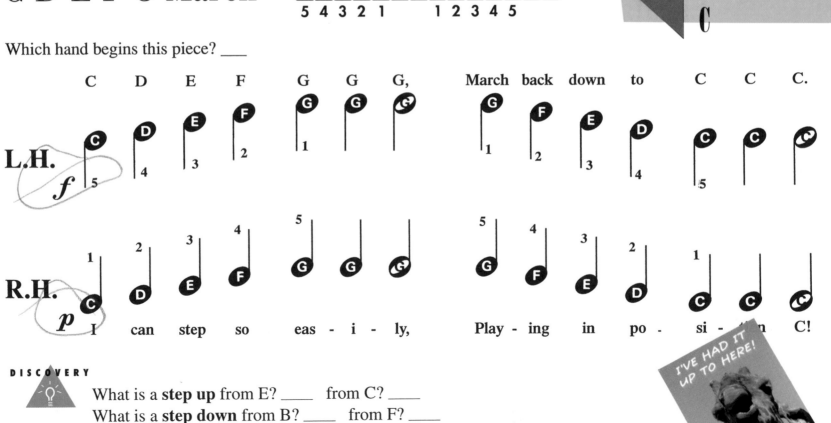

L.H.

C D E F G G G, March back down to C C C.

f 5 4 3 2 1 1 1 2 3 4 5

R.H.

1 2 3 4 5   5 4 3 2 1

p C D E F G G G G F E D C C C

I can step so eas - i - ly, Play - ing in po - si - tion C!

D I S C O V E R Y

What is a **step up** from E? ____ from C? ____
What is a **step down** from B? ____ from F? ____

FF

In music the beats are grouped into *measures*.
Each measure has the same number of beats.
Bar lines divide the music into measures.

Men from Mars

C Position

Circle each bar line in the piece.
How many measures are in *Men from Mars*? ____

R.H. *f*

Three green men from plan - et Mars trav - eled here from quite a - far.

Asked me if I'd feed them, please, so I gave them all green cheese!

L.H.

DISCOVERY For each measure, show your teacher where the music **steps up** , **steps down**, or **repeats**.

Teacher Duet: (Student plays *high* on the keyboard)

Performance p. 8   Theory p. 14   Technique p. 12, 13

Remember *p* is soft, *f* is loud.
These are called **dynamic marks**.

New dynamic mark: *mf* (*mezzo forte*) - moderately (medium) loud

Ode to Joy
(from the *9th Symphony*)

C Position

Ludwig van Beethoven

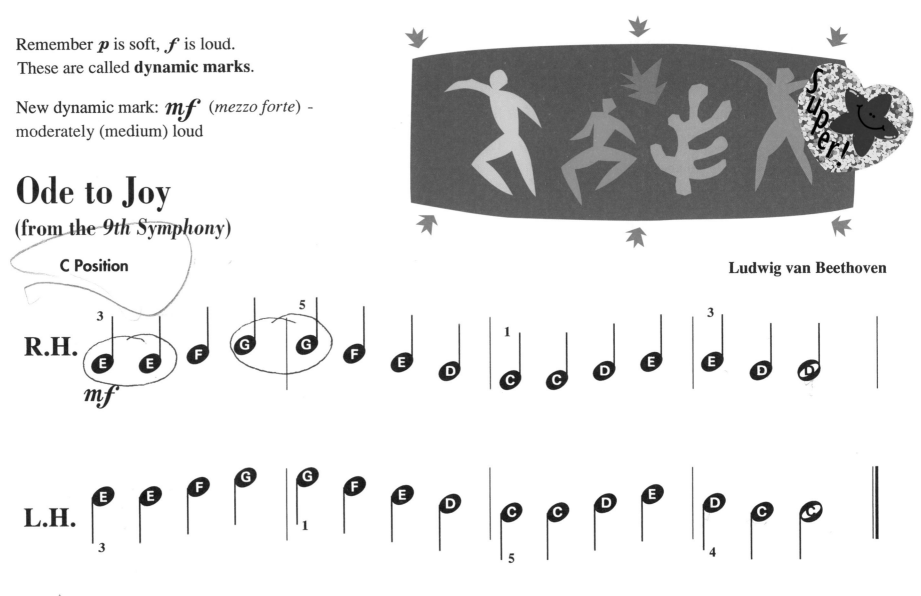

DISCOVERY
This piece uses **steps** and **repeated notes**. Find and circle the 9 pairs of repeated notes. The first two have been done for you.

Teacher Duet: (Student plays *very high* on the keyboard)

L.H.   *mp* *with pedal*

(1) - **thumbs share Middle C**

Notice the R.H. is the same as C Position.
The L.H. is different!

Middle C Position

L.H. · R.H.

(boat illustration)

Partners at C

Eye Check: *Are your eyes on the music and not on your hands?*

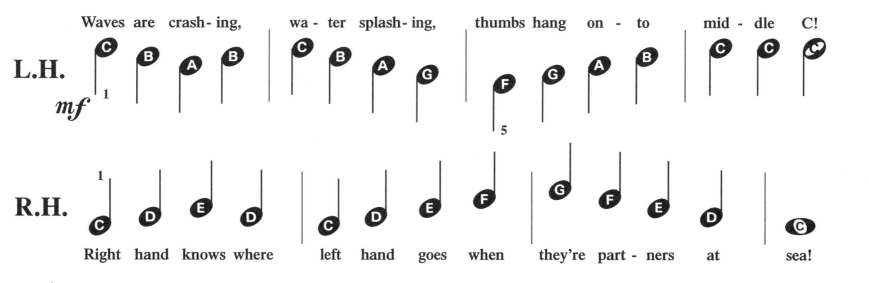

Waves are crash-ing, wa-ter splash-ing, thumbs hang on-to mid-dle C!

L.H. *mf*

R.H.

Right hand knows where left hand goes when they're part-ners at sea!

CREATIVE Can you play this piece with your L.H. starting on a *low* C and
your R.H. starting on a *high* C? Try playing it *forte*, then *mezzo forte*.

Teacher Duet: (Student plays *high* on the keyboard)

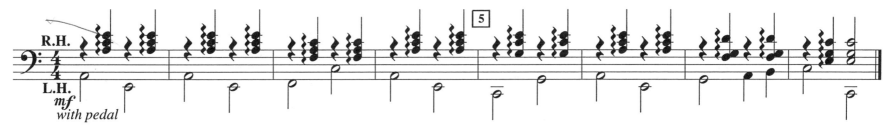

R.H.

L.H.
mf
with pedal

The Dotted Half Note

$\bm{\dot{d}}$ = 3 counts (or beats)
count "1 - 2 - 3"
or "Ta - ah - ah"

$\bm{d}$ + $\bm{d}$ + $\bm{d}$ = $\bm{\dot{d}}$

Hey, Mr. Half Note Dot!
Middle C Position

Hey,	Mis	- ter	Half Note Dot!	Hey,	Mis	ter	Half Note Dot!
When	you	go	1 - 2 - 3,	dance	up	to	Mid - dle C.

L.H. C B A G. G A B C.

mf

R.H. C D E F G F E D C.

| You | sound | like | you've | just | been | danc | - | ing. (2 - 3) |
| We | sound | like | we've | just | been | danc | - | ing. (2 - 3) |

Teacher Duet: (Student plays *low* on the keyboard)   *repeat 8va higher*

FF10

Alouette

C Position

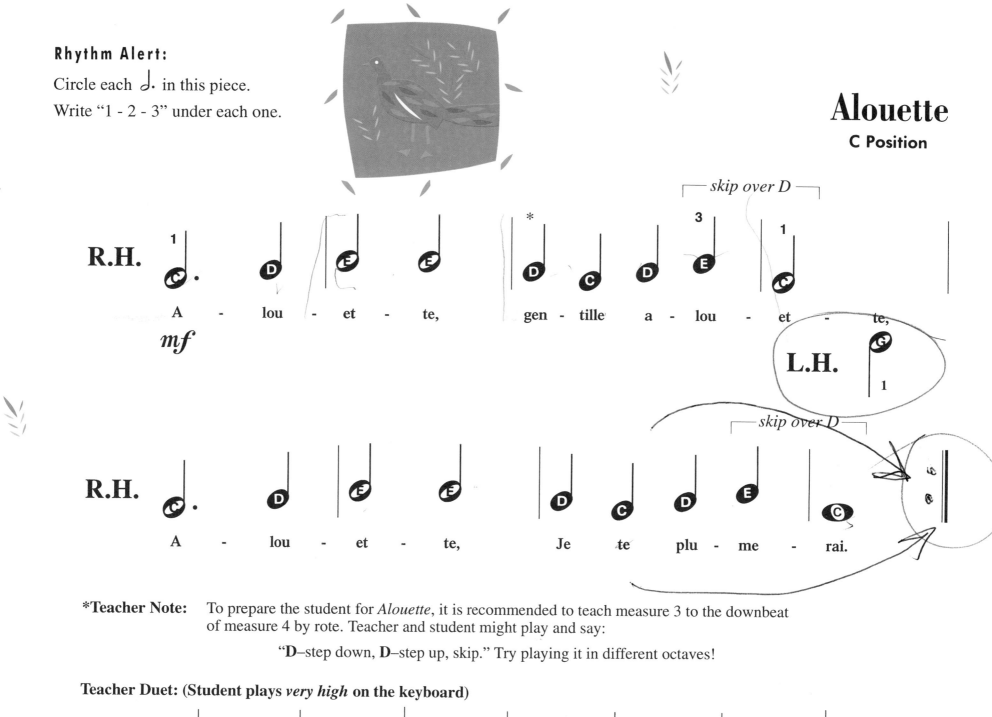

┌─ *skip over D* ─┐

R.H. **1** C. D E E | D C D **3** E | **1** C |

A - lou - et - te, gen - tille a - lou - et - te,

mf

L.H. G **1**

┌─ *skip over D* ─┐

R.H. C. D E E | D C D E | C |

A - lou - et - te, Je te plu - me - rai.

*Teacher Note: To prepare the student for *Alouette*, it is recommended to teach measure 3 to the downbeat of measure 4 by rote. Teacher and student might play and say:

"**D**–step down, **D**–step up, skip." Try playing it in different octaves!

Teacher Duet: (Student plays *very high* on the keyboard)

R.H.

5

L.H. *mp*

Performance p. 11   Theory p. 17   Technique p. 16

The Staff

This is a staff. It has **5 lines** and **4 spaces**.

Point to each line saying its number aloud. Then do the same with each space.

Notes are written **on the lines** or **in the spaces** of the staff.

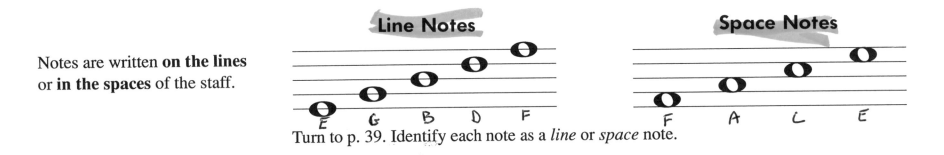

Turn to p. 39. Identify each note as a *line* or *space* note.

The Grand Staff

In piano music we use 2 staffs. Together we call them the **GRAND STAFF**.

The Right Hand usually uses the top staff.

The Left Hand usually uses the bottom staff.

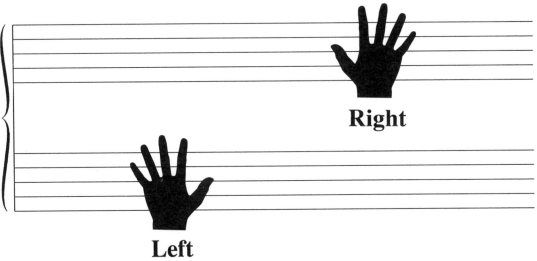

FF1

The Bass Clef and Treble Clef

 This is a **Bass Clef.** (Bass means *low* sounds.)
The bass clef is placed on the bottom staff
and is used to show **notes below Middle C.**

Use your left hand:

Play Middle C and all the notes below while
naming them aloud. These are bass clef notes.

 This is a **Treble Clef.** (Treble means *high* sounds.)
The treble clef is placed on the top staff
and is used to show **notes above Middle C.**

Use your right hand:

Play Middle C and all the notes above while
naming them aloud. These are treble clef notes.

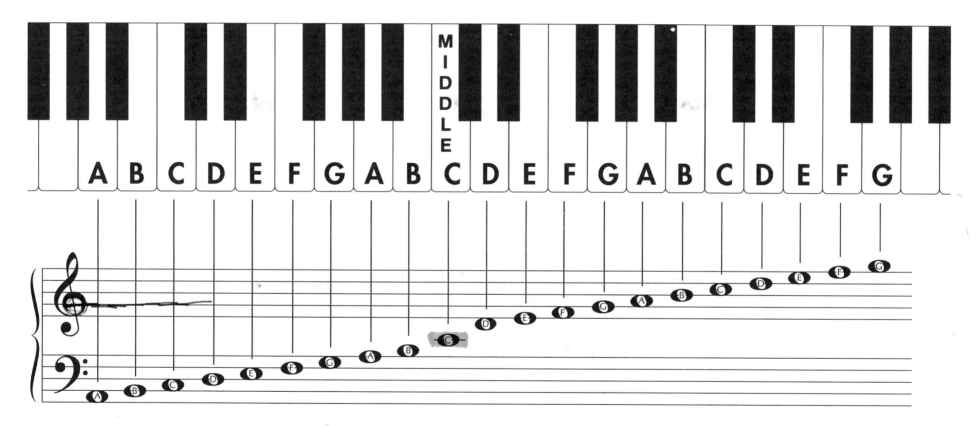

How many times can the music alphabet be written on the staff? Begin at the bottom and count up. _____

Teacher's Note: This is an orientation page only. Students will learn these notes gradually throughout the method.

Learning Middle C

Middle C is the dividing note between the treble clef and bass clef.

It is on a short line between the staffs.

*Watch for the changes in fingering.**

Middle C March

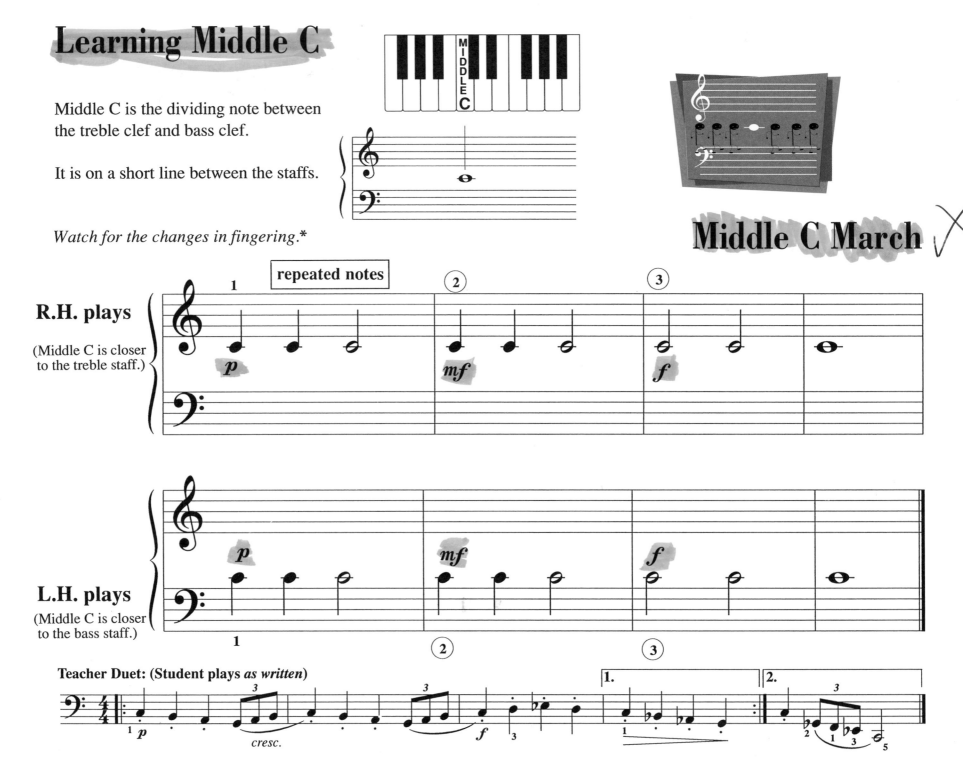

R.H. plays

(Middle C is closer to the treble staff.)

repeated notes

L.H. plays

(Middle C is closer to the bass staff.)

Teacher Duet: (Student plays *as written*)

cresc.

*Teacher's Note: The change of fingering prevents the student from equating a certain note (e.g. Middle C) with a specific finger (e.g. thumb).

Learning Treble G

On the keyboard find the G *above* Middle C (5 notes away). This is called **Treble G**.

Hand Shape Exercise

With R.H. fingers 1 and 5, play back and forth between Middle C and Treble G.

On the staff, **Treble G is written on line 2**.

line 2 **G** →

The treble clef is also called the G clef because it circles around the G line on the staff.

A Ten-Second Song ✓

Circle all the G's in this piece.

Lightly

1 *on* __C__? *(fill in)*

5 *on* __G__? *(fill in)*

mf

I just love to | play this song, | for it's just ten | sec - onds long.
If this song to had | no re - peats, | it would just be so | short and sweet!

DISCOVERY With a colored pencil, trace over the **G line** for the first measure of this piece.
(Your teacher may have you do this for many pieces in the book.)

Teacher Duet: (Student plays *as written*)

R.H.

L.H.

mf

Theory p. 19, 20

075

In this piece Middle C and Treble G are played *at the same time* with the R.H. Notice the notes share the same stem.

Honking Cars ✗ Count!!

Urgently

Beep,   beep,   in   the   streets,   Beep,   beep,   traf - fic   meets.

measure number **5**

Cit - y   sounds   are   all   a - round,   Beep,   honk,   beep!

DISCOVERY How many measures have this rhythm? ♩ ♩ ♩ ___ Can you play this piece looking only at the music?

Teacher Duet: (Student plays *as written*)

FF1

Finger Challenge:

Play **Middle C** with L.H. finger 1, then 2, then 3.
Play **Treble G** with R.H. finger 1, then 2, then 3.
Which fingers play these notes in *Best Friends?* _____

Best Friends

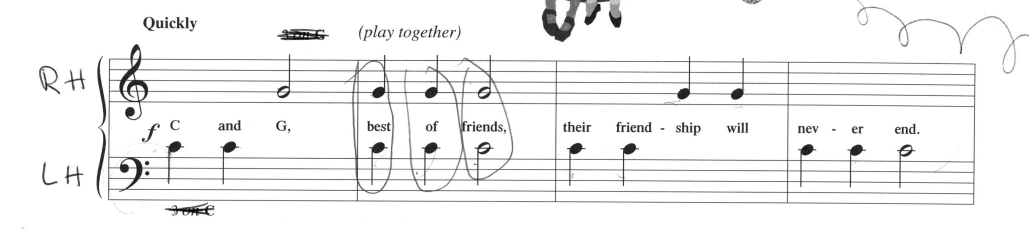

Quickly

(play together)

RH
LH

f C and G, best of friends, their friend - ship will nev - er end.

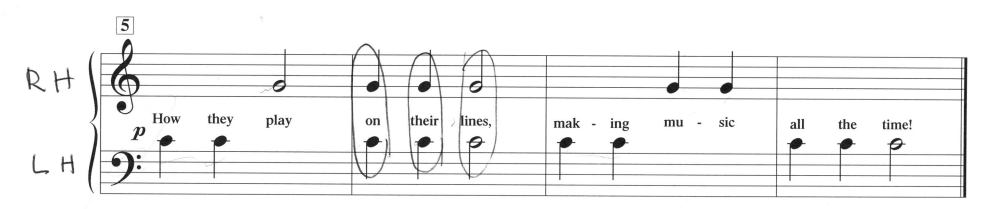

5

RH
LH

p How they play on their lines, mak - ing mu - sic all the time!

DISCOVERY Can you play *Best Friends* using only finger 2 for each hand?
Be sure to play with a firm fingertip!

Teacher Duet: (Student plays *as written*)

f-p on repeat

Performance p. 12   Theory p. 21

Learning Bass F

On the keyboard find the F *below* Middle C (5 notes away).
This is called **Bass F**.

F→

Hand Shape Exercise

With L.H. fingers 1 and 5, play back and forth
between Middle C and Bass F.

On the staff, **Bass F is written on the 2nd line going down**.
The bass clef is also known as the F clef
because the two dots point out the F line on the staff.

Circle all the F's in this piece. (2nd line going down)

Gorilla in the Tree

Count

Happily

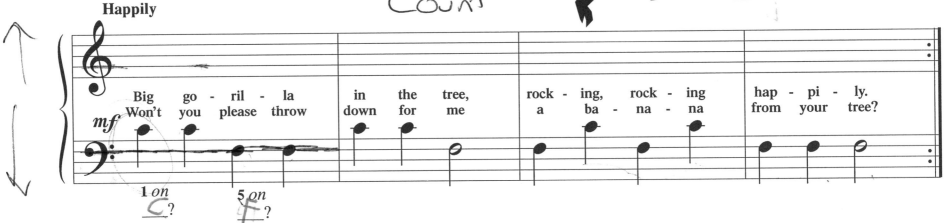

| | Big | go - | ril - la | | in | the | tree, | | rock - | ing, | rock - ing | | hap - | pi - | ly. |
| | Won't | you | please throw | | down | for | me | | a | ba - | na - na | | from | your | tree? |

1 *on*
C?

5 *on*
F?

DISCOVERY With a colored pencil, trace over the **F line** for the first measure of this piece.
(Your teacher may have you trace over the 𝄞 **G line** and 𝄢 **F line** for many pieces in the book.)

Teacher Duet: (Student plays *as written*)

mf

1.

2.

FF1

Finger Challenge:

Play **Bass F** with L.H. finger 1, then 2, 3, 4, and 5.
Which L.H. finger plays **Bass F** in *My Invention*?

My Invention ✗

Like a machine

1 *on*
C?   Count.

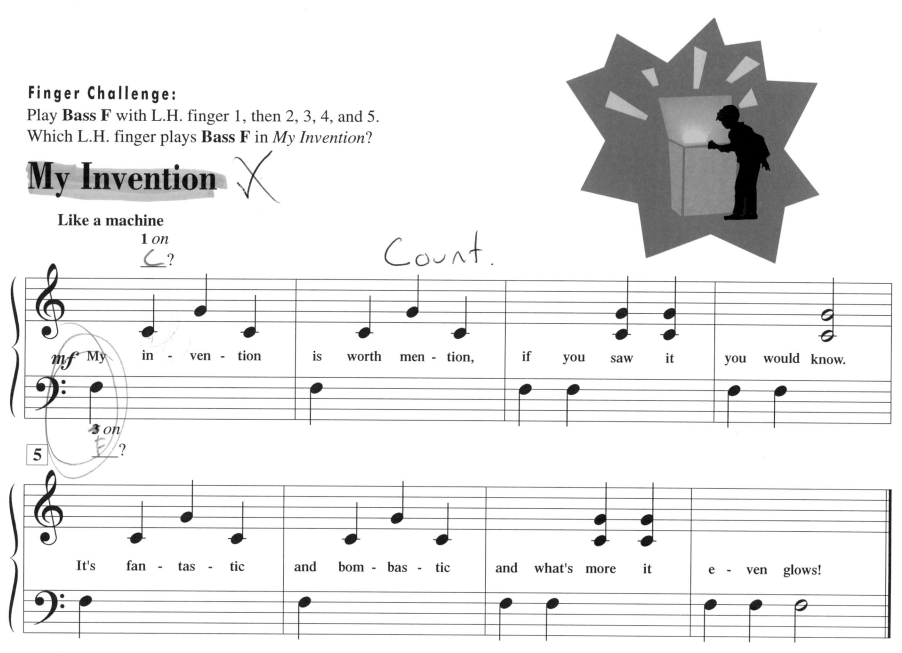

mf My | in - ven - tion | is worth men - tion, | if you saw it | you would know.

3 *on*
F?

It's fan - tas - tic | and bom - bas - tic | and what's more it | e - ven glows!

CREATIVE Compose a longer version of *My Invention* by playing more measures with **Bass F**, **Middle C**, and **Treble G**.
To end, make the invention break down and stop.

Teacher Duet: (Student plays *as written*)

Performance p. 13

Learning D-E-F

D E F

Learn to recognize the 3 notes that
are between Middle C and Treble G.
Which two notes are *space* notes? ___ and ___
Which note is a *line* note? ___

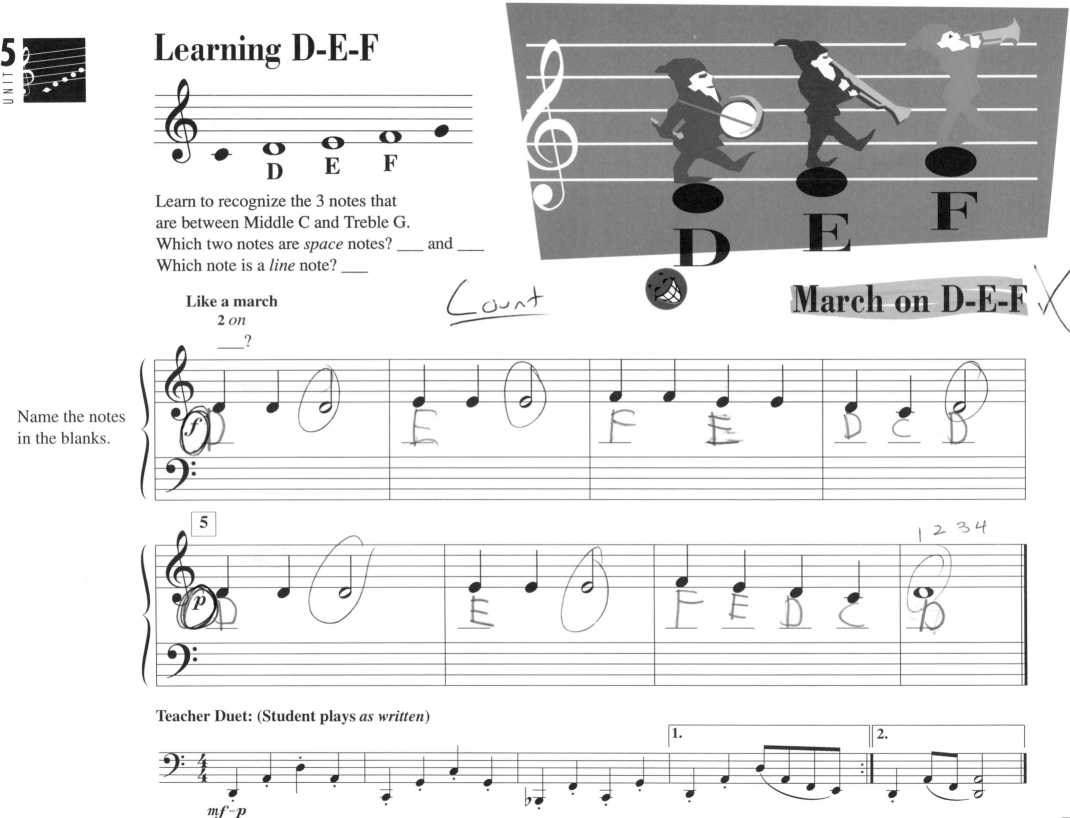

March on D-E-F

Count

Like a march
2 on
___?

Name the notes
in the blanks.

f D __ __ E __ __ F E __ __ D C B

5

p D __ __ E __ F E D C B

1 2 3 4

Teacher Duet: (Student plays *as written*)

1.
2.

mf - p

FF1

Steps on the Staff

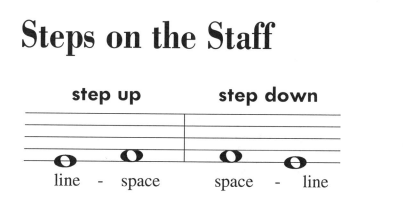

step up	step down
line - space	space - line

When notes move from a **LINE to the next SPACE** or a **SPACE to the next LINE** we **STEP** on the keyboard.
Reminder: A *step* moves to the next finger and the next letter in the musical alphabet. Ex. C-D or D-E (see p. 24 for review)
Before playing *Mister Bluebird*, circle the correct answer for each measure below.

Mister Bluebird

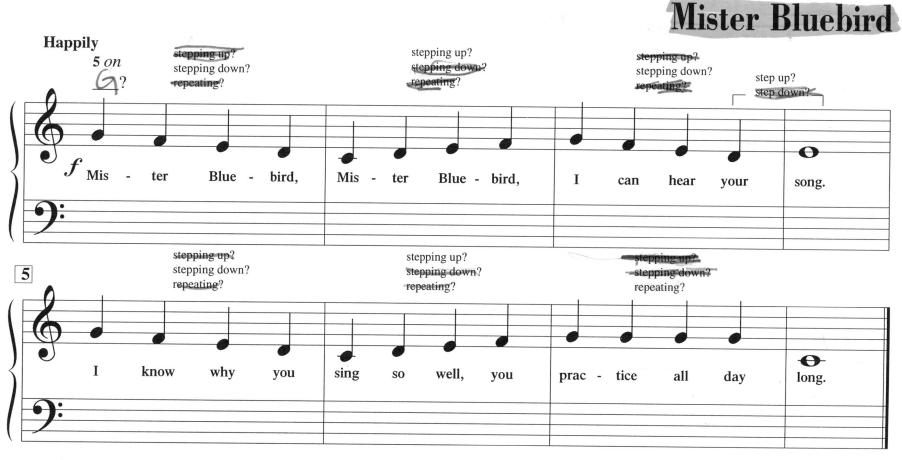

Happily

5 *on* G ?

stepping up?
stepping down?
repeating?

stepping up?
stepping down?
repeating?

stepping up?
stepping down?
repeating?

step up?
step down?

f Mis - ter Blue - bird, Mis - ter Blue - bird, I can hear your song.

5

stepping up?
stepping down?
repeating?

stepping up?
stepping down?
repeating?

stepping up?
stepping down?
repeating?

I know why you sing so well, you prac - tice all day long.

DISCOVERY Can you name each note in this song aloud?

Theory p. 25

The **time signature** tells the number of counts or beats in each measure.
It is always at the beginning of the piece.

4 means 4 counts or beats in a measure.

4 This 4 stands for a quarter note (♩).
It tells us the quarter note gets 1 count.

Circle the time signature in *The Dance Band*.
How many measures are in this piece? __8__
How many counts are in each measure? __4__

The Dance Band

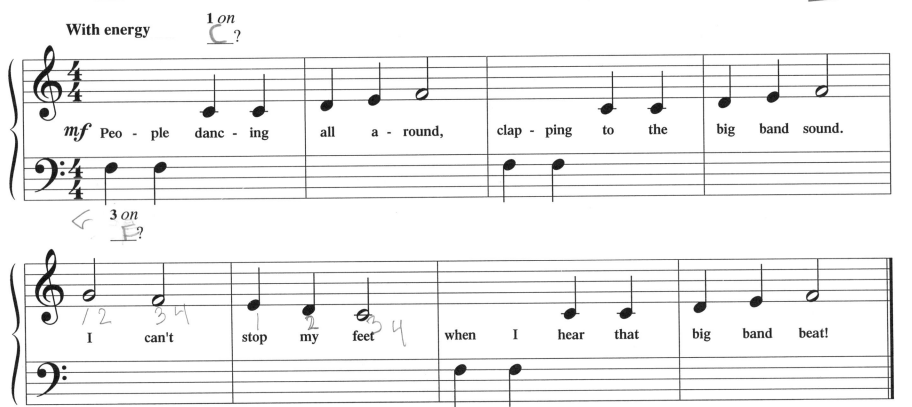

With energy

1 *on*
C?

mf Peo - ple danc - ing | all a - round, | clap - ping to the | big band sound.

3 *on*
E?

I can't | stop my feet | when I hear that | big band beat!

DISCOVERY Name the first note of every measure.

FF

This piece uses a change in fingering for the right hand.*
A circled finger number will help you recognize a change.

Frogs on Logs

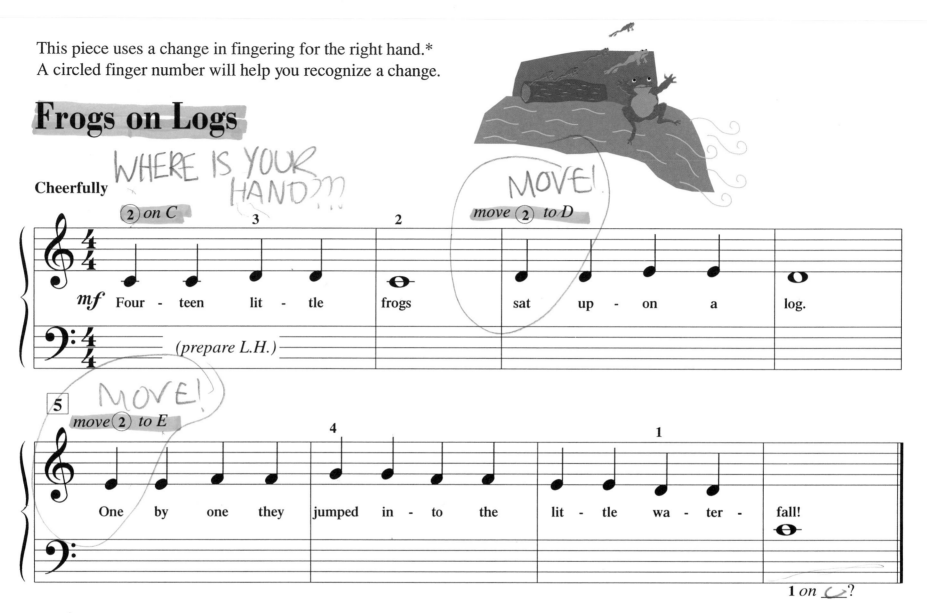

Cheerfully *WHERE IS YOUR HAND???*

② on C   3   2   *MOVE!*   move ② to D

mf Four - teen   lit - tle   frogs   sat   up - on   a   log.

(prepare L.H.)

5   *MOVE!*   move ② to E   4   1

One   by   one   they   jumped   in - to   the   lit - tle   wa - ter -   fall!

*1 on ? *

CREATIVE

Using only C's, compose a special ending to *Frogs on Logs* as they jump into the waterfall. Begin *high* and come down the keyboard.

Teacher Duet: (Student plays *as written*)

R.H.

L.H. *mp*

5

Learning B

UNIT 6

B is a step below Middle C.
B is a space note. It sits on *top* of the bass clef staff.
Circle all the B's in *Let's Play Ball.*

line   space
o B

Let's Play Ball!

With zest

POSITION!!!

(prepare R.H.)

3 on
G ?

f Come on, one and all, won't you grab your bat and ball?

5

1 on
C ?

3

We will have a win - ning team so let's play ball!

DISCOVERY Name each note in this piece aloud.

Teacher Duet: (Student plays *as written*)

mf

42   FF1

New Time Signature

3 means 3 counts or beats in a measure.

4 means the quarter note gets 1 count or beat.

Circle the time signature in *Petite Minuet*.

Petite Minuet

(A minuet is a dance in **3/4** time.)

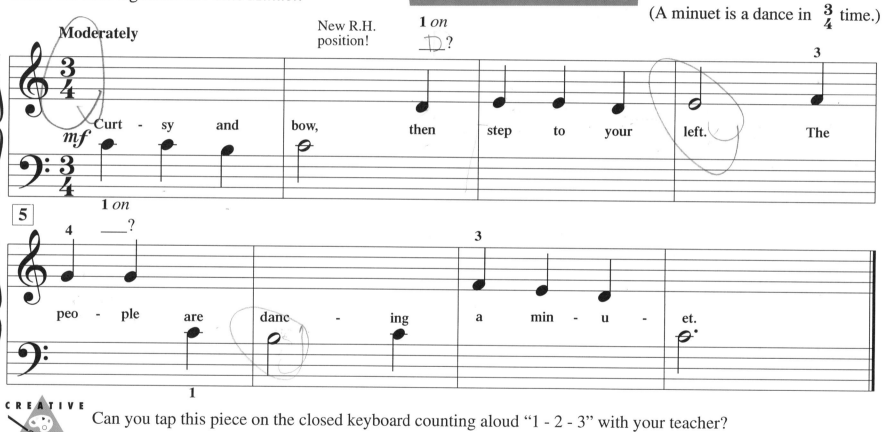

Moderately

New R.H. position!

1 *on* D?

mf

Curt - sy and bow, then step to your left. The

1 *on* ?

5

peo - ple are danc - ing a min - u - et.

CREATIVE

Can you tap this piece on the closed keyboard counting aloud "1 - 2 - 3" with your teacher?
Can you play this piece counting aloud "1 - 2 - 3"?

Teacher Duet: (Student plays *1 octave higher*)

R.H.

L.H. *mp*

Performance p. 18   Theory p. 30, 31, 32

Learning A

A is a line note.
It is the **top line** of the bass staff.
Circle all the A's in *Rodeo*.

line space line
○ A

Rodeo

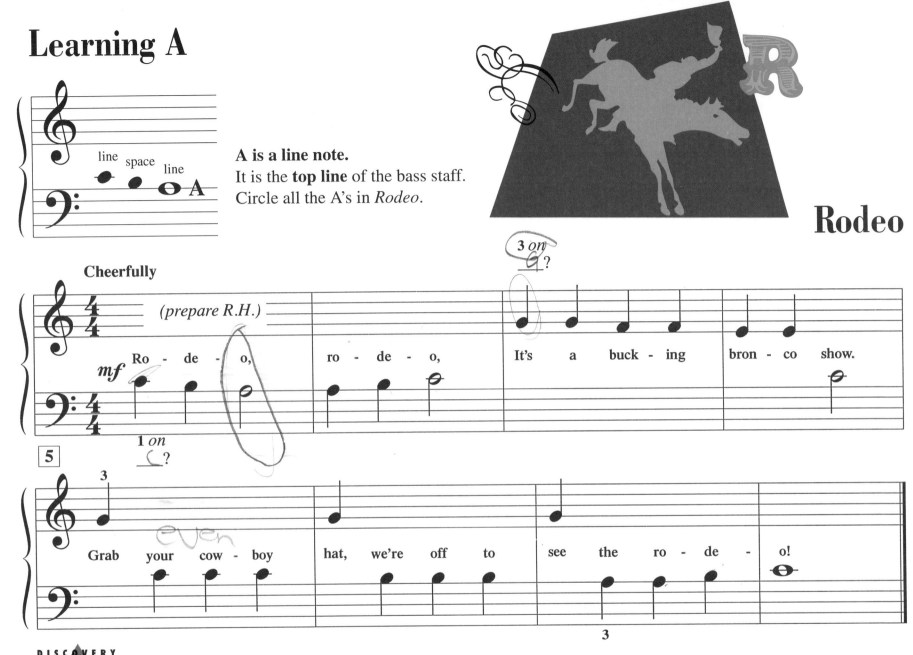

Cheerfully

3 on G?

(prepare R.H.)

mf Ro - de - o, ro - de - o, It's a buck - ing bron - co show.

1 on C?

[5]

Grab your cow - boy hat, we're off to see the ro - de - o!

DISCOVERY Point out all the repeated notes. Then name each note in this piece aloud.

Teacher Duet (Student plays *1 octave higher*)

R.H.

L.H. *mf*

FF

Reading Alert: For each measure, show your teacher where
the music **steps up, steps down,** and **repeats**.
Hint: Be sure to look over the bar lines, also.

Russian Sailor Dance

Quickly

Traditional

DISCOVERY
Where is there an echo in this piece? Show your teacher.

Teacher Duet: (Student plays *1 octave higher*)

Performance p. 19

Learning G

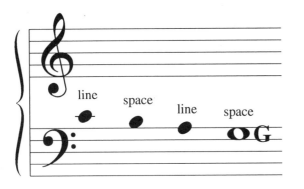

line space line space

o G

G is a space note.
It is the top or **4th space** of the bass staff.

Find and circle all the bass clef G's
in *Come See the Parade!*

Come See the Parade!

Right
Left

Lively   **5** *on* G?
        1 *on* C?

G

𝆒 4/4   𝄢 4/4

f

5   Left   3

mf   Tu - bas   march - ing | down   the   street, | come   see   the   pa - | rade!

𝄢

1 *on* ___?

The student is now ready to choose a book from the *PreTime Piano Series* (see back cover).

FF

9

Bass drum keeps a big bass beat, come see the pa - rade!

⌐ Optional: For solo, play these 2 measures ⌐
    beginning on the next LOWER C.

13

f

G

4

With R.H. fingers 1 and 5, create a short rhythm playing **Middle C** and **Treble G** together.
Can you repeat your rhythm on a higher C and G?

Teacher Duet: (Student plays *1 octave higher*)

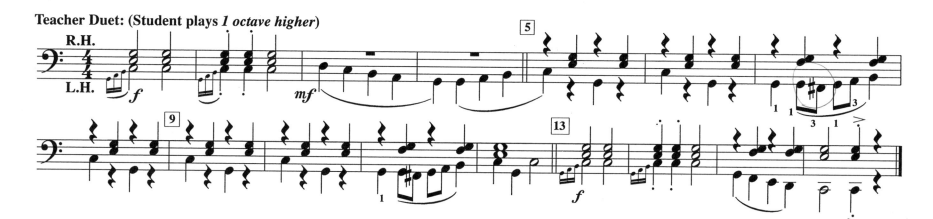

R.H.

L.H. *f* *mf*

5

9 **13** *f*

Performance p. 20, 21   Theory p. 34, 35   Technique p. 21

About Skips

To **SKIP** on the piano: skip a key 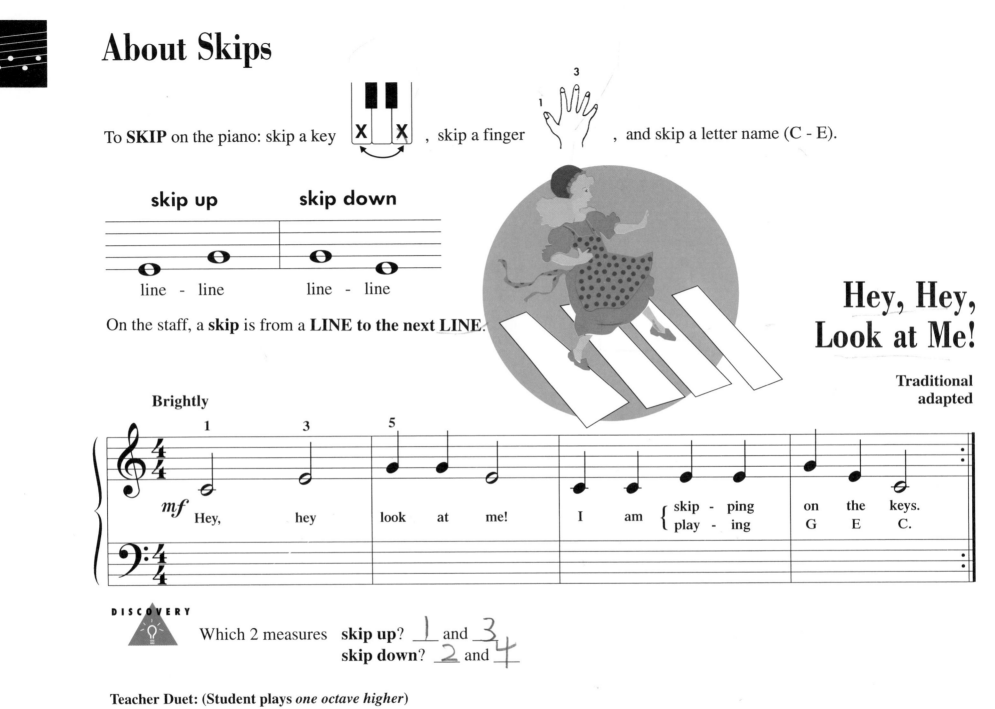 , skip a finger , and skip a letter name (C - E).

skip up   **skip down**

line - line   line - line

On the staff, a **skip** is from a **LINE to the next LINE**.

Hey, Hey, Look at Me!

Traditional adapted

Brightly

mf Hey, hey look at me! I am { skip - ping / play - ing } on the keys. G E C.

DISCOVERY

Which 2 measures **skip up**? 1 and 3
skip down? 2 and 4

Teacher Duet: (Student plays *one octave higher*)

R.H.

L.H.

1.   2.

Allegro

Reading Alert: Circle at least 8 skips in this piece. Hint: Don't forget to look over the bar lines!

(*Allegro* is the Italian word for fast and lively.)

Mauro Giuliani
(1781-1829, Italy)
adapted

Performance p. 23   Theory p. 37

DISCOVERY Circle the time signature. Tell your teacher what it means.

Teacher Duet: (Student plays *1 octave higher*)

More about Skips

Review: A skip is from a line to the next line.

New: A skip is also from a **SPACE to the next SPACE**.

skip up	skip down
space - space	space - space

Elephant Ride

Merrily

2 *on*

When you're on an el - e - phant you sit real - ly high.

4 *on*

5

And you'll have the fin - est view while on your jun - gle ride!

DISCOVERY Which three measures only skip space to space? *measure ___ ___ and ___*

Teacher Duet: (Student plays *1 octave higher*)

R.H.

L.H.

Reading Check: Circle 4 skips which move from **space** to **space**.

Yankee Doodle

Brightly

Traditional American

2 on
___?

4 on
___?

Sing a - long, as I play this song: Yan - kee Doo - dle went to town

rid - ing on a po - ny, Stuck a feath - er in his cap and called it mac - a - ron - i!

CREATIVE Hold the right foot (damper) pedal down for measures 1-4. Your teacher will show you how.

Teacher Duet: (Student plays *1 octave higher*)

R.H.

L.H.

mp

75

Performance p. 25   Theory p. 39   Technique p. 24, 25

Learning Bass C

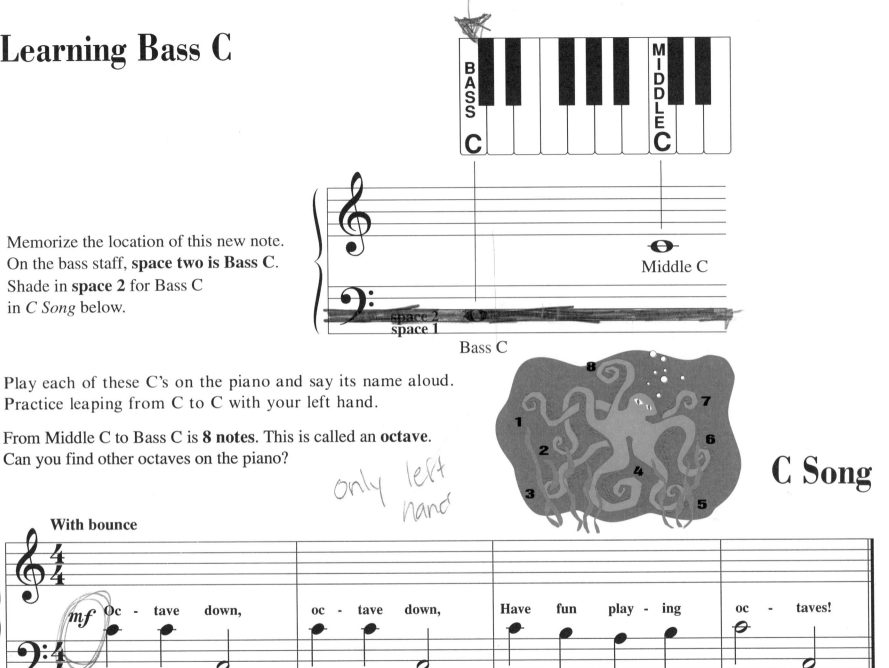

Memorize the location of this new note.
On the bass staff, **space two is Bass C**.
Shade in **space 2** for Bass C
in *C Song* below.

Middle C

space 2
space 1

Bass C

Play each of these C's on the piano and say its name aloud.
Practice leaping from C to C with your left hand.

From Middle C to Bass C is **8 notes**. This is called an **octave**.
Can you find other octaves on the piano?

only left hand

C Song

With bounce

mf Oc - tave down,   oc - tave down,   Have fun play - ing   oc - taves!

1   5
(leap don't stretch)

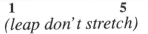 **DISCOVERY** Does the stem go up or down on Bass C? _____
(This is done so the stem doesn't extend below the staff.)

C Position

You have already learned the circled notes.

In C position, the L.H. has 2 new notes. What are they? ___ and ___

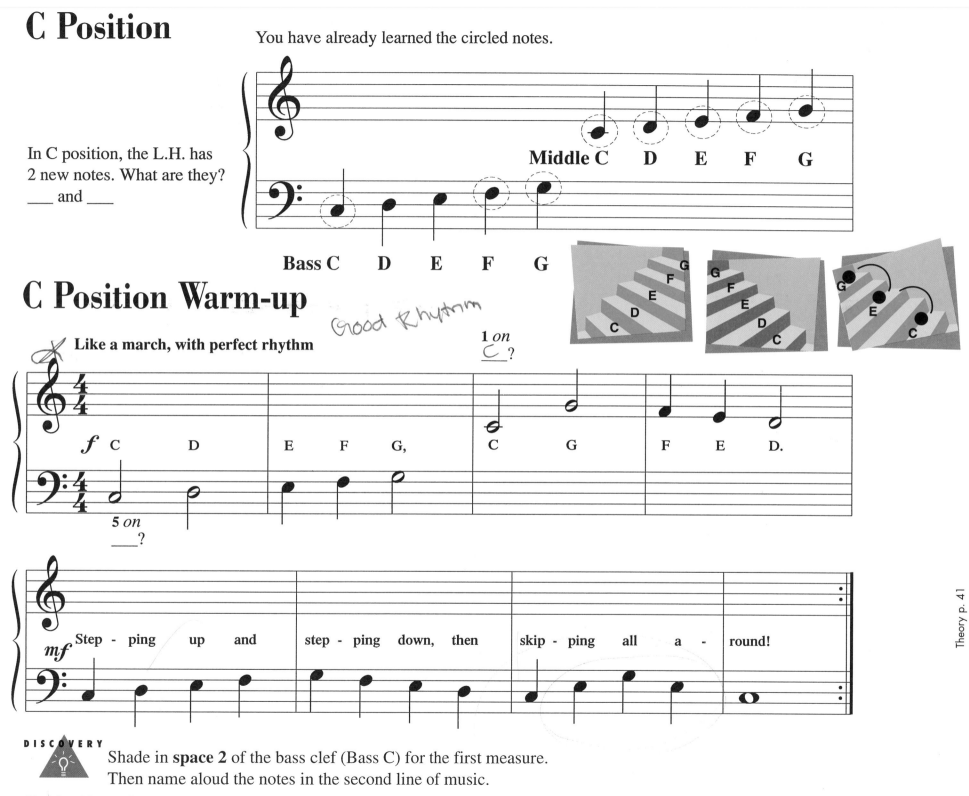

Middle C   D   E   F   G

Bass C   D   E   F   G

C Position Warm-up

Good Rhythm

Like a march, with perfect rhythm

1 on C ?

f C   D   E   F   G,   C   G   F   E   D.

5 on ___ ?

mf Step - ping   up   and   step - ping   down,   then   skip - ping   all   a - round!

DISCOVERY

Shade in **space 2** of the bass clef (Bass C) for the first measure.
Then name aloud the notes in the second line of music.

Teacher Note: The student may benefit from shading in bass clef space 2 (Bass C) for other pieces in the book.

Theory p. 41

53

Reading Alert: Circle 2 skips in the second line of music. Hint: Be sure to look over the bar lines!

Copy Cat

C Position

Happily

Ev - ery lit - tle thing I do, left hand has to cop - y, too.
For - te is my next com - mand! "Right hand, you can't fool this hand!"

If the left hand's not the same means that it will lose the game.
Left hand, you're quite good at that. "That's 'cause I'm a cop - y cat!"

CREATIVE Make up a 2-measure melody with your R.H.
Have your L.H. "copy" it (play back the same melody).

Teacher Duet: (Student plays *1 octave higher***)**

54

Grandmother

C Position

counting

Cheerfully

Traditional

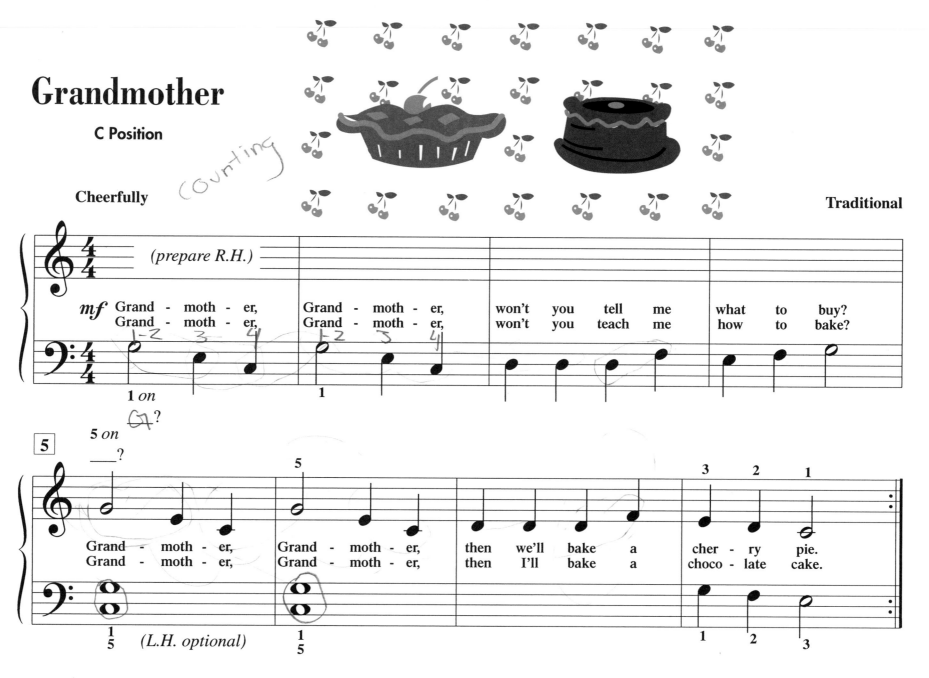

DISCOVERY Point out the two measures that use only **steps**. Are you stepping up or stepping down?

Teacher Duet: (Student plays *1 octave higher*)

Performance p. 27   Theory p. 43   Technique p. 27

The Tie

A **tie** is a curved line connecting 2 notes on the same line or space.
It means the note will be played *once* but held for the length of both notes combined.

Lemonade Stand

Name the position. _____

Rhythm Alert: Can you tap this piece on the closed piano lid counting aloud "1 - 2 - 3" with your teacher?

Hint: Be sure to tap with the correct hand!

Teacher Duet: (Student plays *1 octave higher*)

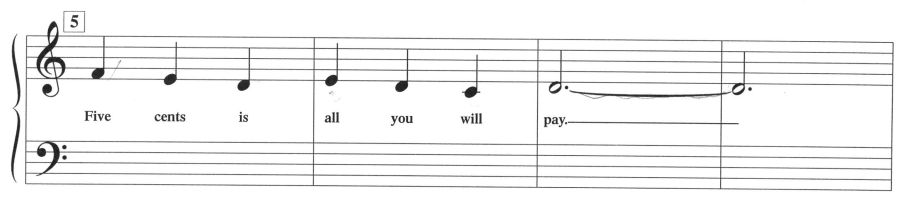

Five cents is all you will pay.

No bet - ter lem - on - ade can be found.

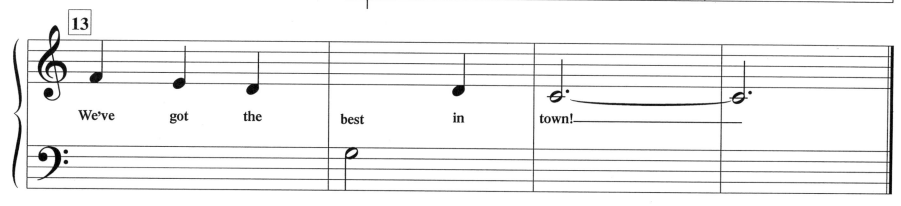

We've got the best in town!

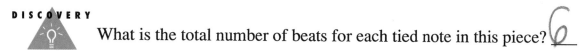

DISCOVERY

What is the total number of beats for each tied note in this piece? 6

All My Friends

Name the position. _C_

Rhythm Alert: Circle each tie in the music.

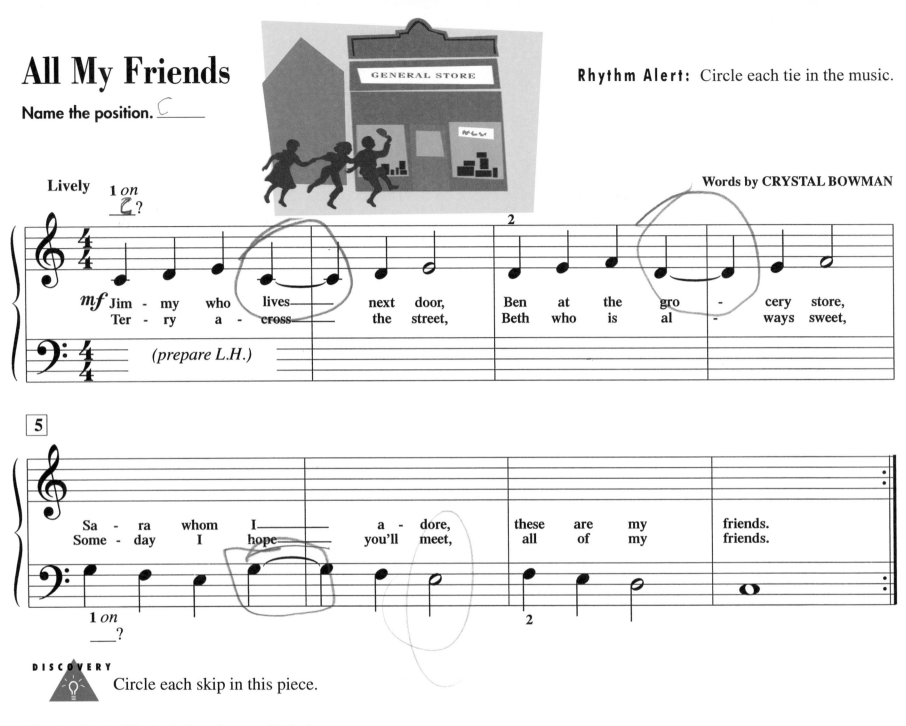

Words by CRYSTAL BOWMAN

Lively

mf Jim - my who lives next door, Ben at the gro - cery store,
Ter - ry a - cross the street, Beth who is al - ways sweet,

(prepare L.H.)

Sa - ra whom I a - dore, these are my friends.
Some - day I hope you'll meet, all of my friends.

DISCOVERY Circle each skip in this piece.

Teacher Duet: (Student plays *1 octave higher*)

58

Bells of Great Britain

Name the position. _____

Special bells effect:

Hold down the right foot (damper) pedal through the entire piece.

Describe the sound to your teacher.

Joyfully

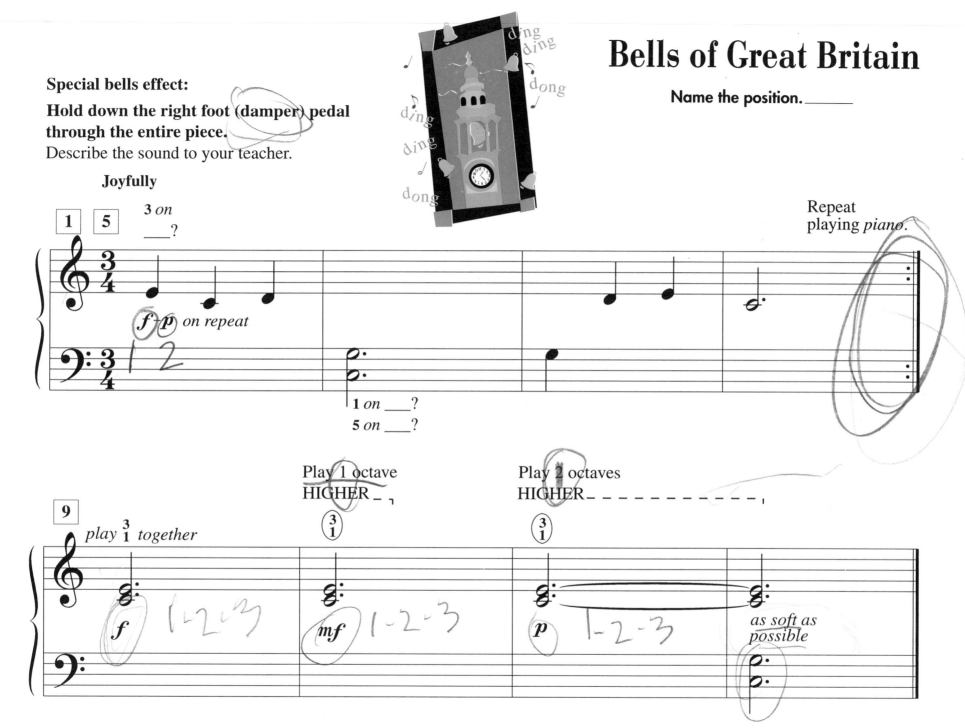

3 *on* ___?

1 *on* ___?
5 *on* ___?

f - p on repeat

Repeat playing *piano*.

Play 1 octave
HIGHER

Play 2 octaves
HIGHER

play 3/1 *together*

f 1-2-3

mf 1-2-3

p 1-2-3

as soft as possible

CREATIVE

Hold the right foot (damper) pedal down and play skips with R.H. fingers **1** and **3** played together.
Play *high* on the piano and listen to the bell-like sounds!

Music often has moments of silence. These are shown by **rests**.

quarter rest ↕ = *silence* for 1 beat

Set a steady beat with your teacher by tapping on your lap.
Together, chant and tap the "cheer" below.
On the rests, **feel the beat but do not tap or speak.**

Go	Team	Let's	Win
Go	Team	Let's	Win
↕	Team	Let's	Win
↕	↕	Let's	Win
↕	↕	↕	Win!

Our Team

Steady and strong

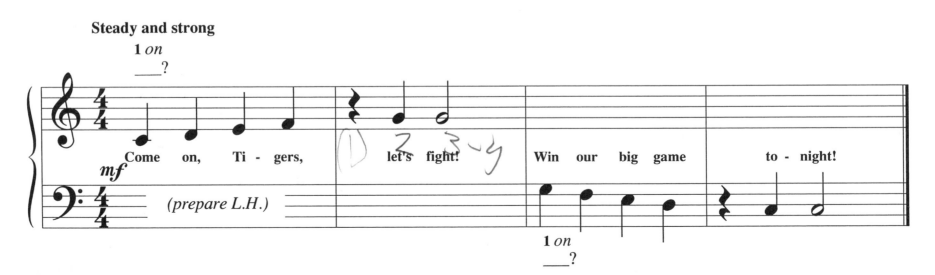

1 *on*
____?

Come on, Ti - gers, let's fight! Win our big game to - night!

mf

(prepare L.H.)

1 *on*
____?

Reading Alert: Circle each skip in this piece.

Once There Was a Princess

Name the position. _____

Bright and fast

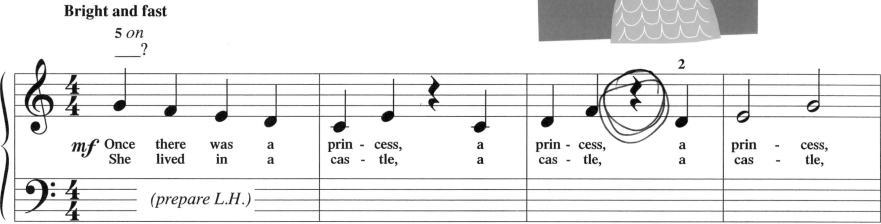

5 *on*
___?

mf Once there was a   prin - cess,   a   prin - cess,   a   prin - cess,
    She lived in a   cas - tle,   a   cas - tle,   a   cas - tle,

(prepare L.H.)

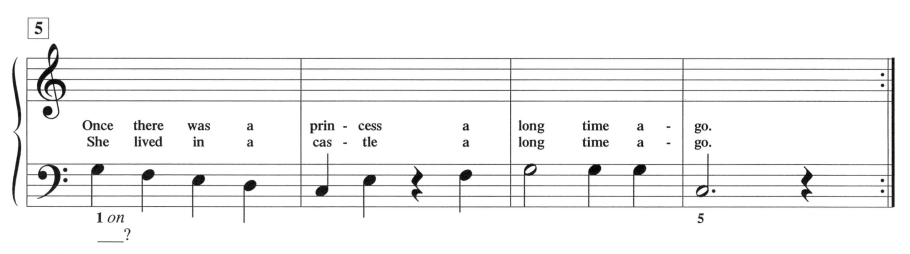

Once there was a   prin - cess   a   long time a - go.
She lived in a   cas - tle   a   long time a - go.

1 *on*
___?

DISCOVERY How many measures have a quarter rest? ___

Teacher Duet: (Student plays *1 octave higher*)

R.H.

L.H. *mp*

Performance p. 30   Theory p. 46   Technique p. 31

The Bugle Boys

Name the position. _____

Marching briskly

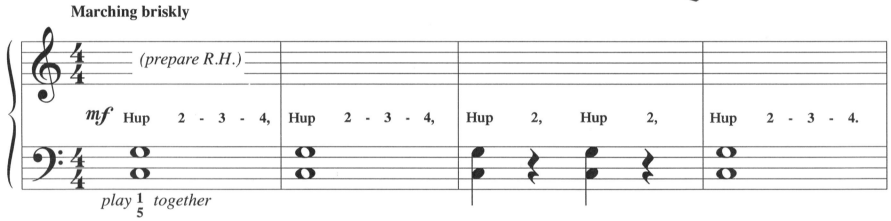

(prepare R.H.)

mf Hup 2 - 3 - 4, Hup 2 - 3 - 4, Hup 2, Hup 2, Hup 2 - 3 - 4.

play $\frac{1}{5}$ *together*

5

1

f See them proud - ly march - ing, let's all give a cheer.

leave down

FF

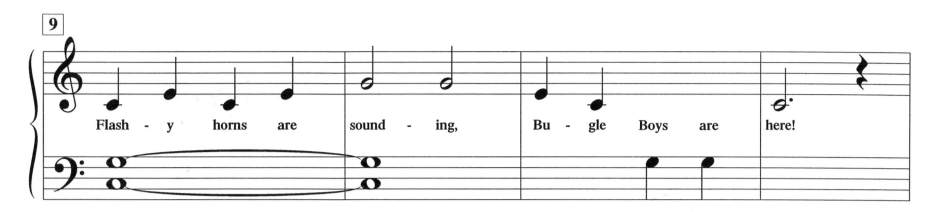

9 Flash - y horns are sound - ing, Bu - gle Boys are here!

13 _Repeat from here._

Play **3** times gradually getting softer and softer.
Move the L.H. 1 octave lower for each repeat!

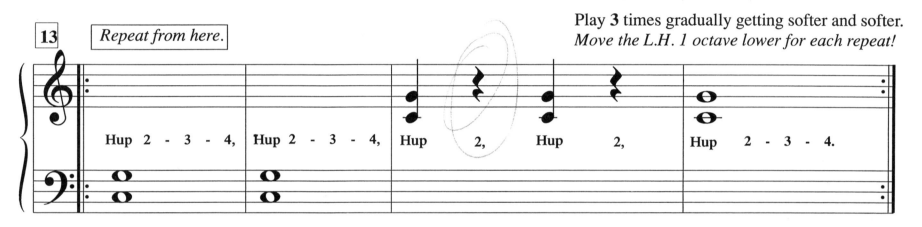

Hup 2 - 3 - 4, Hup 2 - 3 - 4, Hup 2, Hup 2, Hup 2 - 3 - 4.

CREATIVE This piece uses only three letter names. Name them. ___ ___ ___ Make up your own march using notes C-E-G. Call it "Congratulations March." You've finished the book!

Teacher Duet: (Student plays _as written_)

Play 3 times getting softer with each repeat!

Technique p. 32   Theory p. 47, 48   Performance p. 32

Certificate of Achievement

CONGRATULATIONS TO

Shaam Kanji

(Your Name)

You have completed **PIANO ADVENTURES® PRIMER LEVEL** and are now ready for

Piano Adventures® Lesson Book Level 1
Piano Adventures® Theory Book Level 1
Piano Adventures® Performance Book Level 1
Piano Adventures® Technique & Artistry Book Level 1

Teacher _____

Date 2-22-10